As if in a Distant Dream

A collection of poetry

Mark Schardine

ISBN- 978-1-7333822-2-9

Published by:

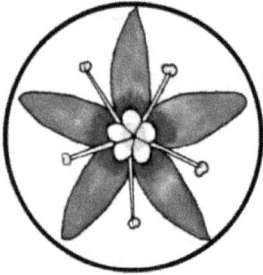

Blue Jade Press, LLC

Blue Jade Press, LLC
Vineland, NJ 08360
www.bluejadepress.com

Introduction

Poets experiment with the use of forms. They search for a means to condense ideas and to present them, not only with clarity, but also with refinement. As heirs to the great traditions of poetry, we understand the need to learn from the past, also to find new ways to express our ideas, to take familiar forms and adapt them to the challenges we face as we write.

The Internet site fanstory.com offers insight into many diverse poetic forms, among them the Japanese forms of haiku and senryū. These forms include three lines: the first consists of five syllables, the second of seven syllables, and the third of five. The strictness and brevity of the forms require careful thought and meditation in order to bring ideas into focus.

Poets can be creative with these strict forms in a number of different ways. A collection of three-line untitled poems can present ideas related to a particular theme, or be random, with one poem after another offering its unique viewpoint. These short poems can work together for a larger piece, or can be presented individually as complete poems. A poet can also create a poem with several three-line stanzas, each of which must play its role in the poem, and choose to give a title to the poem.

Any poetic form can seem very limiting, since it disallows lines a poet might have chosen. The initial efforts concentrate on learning the rules and how to work within them. With practice, the rules become less a set of confines and more of a series of guideposts. They sharpen the focus, turn attention to the essential ideas of the poem, and provide precise instructions to transform a few words into a meaningful poem.

A poem written in one of these forms can be read in a short amount of time, but its few words can express a great variety of ideas. This allows the reader to spend time reflecting and considering different ways of understanding and interpreting them. We can return to a poem that has greatly affected us, and recognize how each reading of it can offer new insight.

Chapters

The Sea

Predators

Sharks cross the ocean
Thousands of miles each year
Never a respite

Fins move back and forth
Pushing onward through the depths
Never under strain

They know the sea well
Can navigate and hunt prey
In all conditions.

Man with his machines
Radar, sonar, and the rest
Cannot find his way

He ventures off course
Runs aground, or into storms
Vanquished by the sea

He can only hope
To understand what he sees
And build new machines

While sharks swim onward
Unaware of man's efforts
To subdue the sea.

The Sea Before Us

Man looks to the sea
Outward, into the distance
Toward the horizon.

He cannot stand still
Theorizing, pondering,
He must venture forth.

Building boats and ships
He risks all to discover
Lands beyond the sea.

Yet under the waves
The sea guards secrets, holding
Fast to its treasures.

Man must plunge headlong
Beneath the surface, into
Depths far from sunlight.

His ships will founder
Man struggles yet will succumb,
Sunk without a trace.

Mankind will persist
Sailing farther in his ships
Riding out fierce storms.

Down to the bottom
He dives, exploring the depths,
Uncovers secrets.

Though the costs will mount
The men, the ships, lost at sea
Yet he will go forth.

Memories of Biarritz
La mer vivante

Waves crash on the beach
White foam spreads to cover sand
And then vanishes.

The breezes pick up,
Cresting waves far out to sea.
The flags flap briskly.

Surfers watch for troughs
Leap up, secure their balance
Zig-zag to the beach.

Jumping below waves
Swimmers head into currents
Letting them flow past.

Twenty meters down
Divers sway with the water
Above speckled rocks.

Aboard pleasure boats
Tourists hold on to railings
While viewing the shore.

Lifeguards hear reports
Fair weather, winds blowing in,
Calming by nightfall.

As yellow flags fly,
We hear a shrill whistle sound
Another rescue.

Memories of Biarritz
La mer et ses dangers

Waves crash on the beach
White foam spreads to cover sand
And then vanishes.

The breezes pick up,
Cresting waves far out to sea.
The flags flap briskly.

Surfers watch for troughs
Leap up, secure their balance
Zig-zag to the beach.

Jumping below waves
Swimmers head into currents
Letting them flow past.

Twenty meters down
Divers sway with the water
Above speckled rocks.

Aboard pleasure boats
Tourists hold on to railings
While viewing the shore.

Lifeguards hear reports
Fair weather, winds blowing in,
Calming by nightfall.

As yellow flags fly,
We hear a shrill whistle sound
The sea claims victims.

Haiku Inspired by the Sea

I

The waves and currents
Pulsating, pushing the sea
In ceaseless motion.

II

Blue sharks cross the sea
Covering great distances
To find weakened prey.

III

The grouper looks calm
Placidly swimming along
Then snatches its prey.

IV

The octopus sits
Alert, blending its colors
Soon to shoot away.

V

The winds gather strength
Seagulls with their outstretched wings
Can drift in the air.

VI

Both eyes on one side
The flounder hides with colors
Mimicking the sand.

VII

The ocean retreats
Revealing a sandy floor
With half-buried shells.

VIII

Created by winds
Waves crest, crash and push forward
Masses of white foam.

IX

Drawing massive nets
The trawler hauls in fish swarms
Then tosses back scraps.

Theft

Scavenging seagulls
Patrol above the boardwalk
Arrange an assault.

Startled beachgoers
See their hot dogs fly away
Bun fragments remain.

Seasons

Winter

December's Onset

Harsh glaring sunlight
Strikes through cold dry windless air
Into bare forests.

The southwestern sky
Dotted with wandering crows
Lets light fade slowly.

A pale slim half moon
Weakly mimics the sun's course
Casts stark strong shadows.

Early December

Slicing from the north
Cold winds strike hands, faces, necks,
Catch us unaware.

Dry brown leaves lie still,
Remain in front of a hedge,
Slowly smother grass.

An early sunset
Precedes a sickle's descent
Only stars give light.

Remembering Jacques Prévert

Like leaves in the wind
Memories fade from our eyes,
Pushed slowly away.

Yet the thoughts remain,
The north wind brings with the cold
A song of past love.

Blighted Landscape

Barren skies and earth
Give no signs of a harvest
Nor nourishing rain.

On leafless branches
Mushrooms spread to soften wood
As roots slowly rot.

Meager Vestiges

On dark, barren fields
An old man surveys bare trees,
Dry leaves, wilted grass.

Sparrows overhead
Have finished foraging here
Nothing remains now

Save rocks, sand, clay, dust,
Dull, gray, brown, inanimate,
Trod by tired feet.

All harvests are done
This earth will yield no more fruit
His eyes stare blankly.

Images of Winter

Brown leaves lie about
After autumn sunlight fades
And winter begins.

Gray clouds overhead
Cover the sky with twilight
Until darkness falls.

A winter day ends
Silence holds sway, no birds sing
No breeze stirs the air.

No stars overhead
No moon reflecting sunlight
Only clouds and mists.

The earth lies quiet
Motionless under calm air
Gives faint breaths of life.

Echoes of Paul Verlaine

Gray winter drizzle
Falls on spirit and heart
As it strikes rooftops.

Tears form in my eyes
No words come to give insight,
To explain my grief.

My sorrow remains
Without cause, yet persistent
To give more sorrow.

Startling Change

Fickle winter winds
Bring warmth, slow down, hesitate,
Then send bitter cold.

Early Snow

A soundless morning:
Snowflakes slowly reach the ground
Soft plush carpets rise.

Above the white earth
Gray skies let more snowflakes fall
Drift slowly downward.

No birds fly about
Snowflakes dominate the air
Impose their silence.

A Soundless Tempest

A soundless tempest
Muffles all, forms deep snow mounds
White splattered branches.

Drifting far afield
We cannot see the road home
Weary feet must halt.

Lengthy wanderings
Ignoring compass, maps, signs
Gray clouds' curtain drawn.

Snowflakes keep falling
Gentle, subtle, elegant
Erase our footprints.

Slowly, life runs out.
Shivering yields to fatigue
Eyes close one last time.

Haiku Inspired by Winter

I

With gusts from the north
December's winds gather strength
Whip signs back and forth.

II

Skies darken early
Cold air belies the bright moon
Frost forms on brown earth.

III

A clear winter dawn
Reveals bright, yet feeble light
That meets frigid air.

IV

The hard frozen earth
Covered with brown wilted grass
Greets the falling snow.

V

Bright winter full moon
Shines its light on barren fields
With dry stalks and leaves.

VI

A thin ice sheet forms
On the surface of the lake
A fragile layer.

VII

Gray cloud-covered skies
Form a curtain of twilight
Hide sun, moon and stars.

VIII

On calm winter days
The wind whispers, sings softly
Hints of snow to come.

IX

Winter traveler
Face to the north wind, trudges
To make his way home.

Winter Moon

Shrouded, hovering,
Calmly shines through the pale sky
Mirroring the snow.

A crow's sharp profile
Stands among craggy branches
Soon his wings will spread.

Mild February Day

Warm southerly gusts
Disperse clouds, fog, dampness, cold
Unveil bright sunlight.

Gray puddles reflect
Winter cold yields this moment
Of brown earth, blue skies.

The winds will slacken
Lose their strength, come to a halt
Cold air will return.

Late Winter Scene

Miles from water
Seagulls drift to the city
Gather to forage.

Amid parking lots
Wild birds can search for food
Pick up man's refuse.

Spring

Rainfall in March

Early spring showers
Slowly soak into the ground
Watering the roots.

Trees gather their strength,
Warmth and water awaken
Dormant energy.

Evening in Early March

The air remains warm
The longer day still gives light
Nature awakens.

On the muddy ground
As yet quite cold to the touch
Timid sprouts emerge.

Birds' songs warble out
Calls and replies in the trees
Announce renewal.

Water gurgles forth
Brooks swell from trickle to flood
As ice melts away.

Cold north winds still blow
But their force diminishes,
Slowly giving way.

Storm at the Equinox

Forming in the west
Gray massing clouds cover the sky
Breezes start swirling.

Rain drops pelt the earth
Lightning bolts strike metal poles
Gusts snap budded twigs.

After clouds have cleared
Sunlight streams in from the west
A rainbow's arc forms.

Vernal Apparition

I, the swift south wind
Warming, soothing, caressing,
Coax you to wander.

Soft whispering sounds
Gentle calm smooth melodies
Lead you far from home.

Over verdant fields
Allowing me to push you
You venture forth.

Winter forgotten
You can see blossoms emerge
I rush farther north.

Clouds come in my wake
Dark-gray lightning-streaked massive
Strive across the sky.

All my force unleashed
I catch you far from shelter
Raindrops pelt your head.

A Meadow in April

Spring bursts forth with life
Dormant energy awakes
In songs and blossoms.

Daffodils, tulips
Nightingales, robins, blue jays
Welcome the sun's warmth.

Yellow, gold, orange
Warbling, chirping, in concert
Insects buzz, chime in.

Easter Flowers

Pale white daffodils
Completely unstained petals
Stand on muddy ground.

Violets

Beneath daffodils
Their forceful rich deep color
Must asset itself.

Not to be concealed
Alert eyes quickly see them
Amid all others.

These tiny blossoms
Arranged above heart-shaped leaves
Let fragrances drift.

Black-yellow striped bees
Hasten to claim their treasure
Inhale, poke, seize, gulp.

Summer

Summer Evening

Brightly lit tree trunks
Stand in contrast to green leaves
Light brown hues come forth.

Birds' songs are still heard
But buzzing intensifies
Insects lurk, clamor.

Outdoor dinners end
Scents linger from thick grilled steaks
Guests recline, content.

A half-moon rises
Charcoal glows, gives off more smoke
Candle light dances.

July Night

In calm humid air
No breeze stirs leafy trees
Summer heat remains.

The insects' singing
Intensifies, defies the dark
Weary, listless night.

Storm clouds hide the stars.
Onto this torpid midnight
Lightning will burst forth.

Haiku Inspired by Summer

I

Long bright evenings
Sunlight streams from west-northwest
Breezes drift about.

II

Pointed pin oak leaves
Rest atop lofty branches
Like spurs in the sun.

III

Clover-dotted lawns
Purple martins perch near me
An eastern wind sighs.

IV

Small growling brown dog
Barks angrily through a fence
Menaces a boy.

V

Gray skies in late June
Dim the sun behind dampness
Dense curtain of mist.

VI

Dark brown mud patches
Standing water, gray pebbles
Deeply pressed footprints.

VII

Dark green maple leaves
Rustling in the afternoon
Feel the wind's caress.

VIII

Last night's thunderstorm
Lets this morning's soaked grass blades
Glisten in the sun.

IX

Birds' soft melodies
Fade before insects' buzzing
Dominates the night.

Mild Weather Today

A cool north wind blows
Assuaging the bright sunlight
While dispelling clouds.

After the solstice
Under a generous sun
Summer heat relents.

A Week-Long Heat Wave

An afternoon sun
Heats up placid, humid air
As mosquitoes buzz.

We become languid
Sweat beads drip down our faces
After morning work.

Slowly the sun drifts
Westward, as air absorbs heat
Blurring our vision.

August Saturday in Spring Lake

Cool winds, warm waters
Swimmers ride on gentle waves
Navigating forth.

Undulating forms
Peaks and troughs in procession
Move in their rhythm.

Calmly but with force,
The ocean sways in the breeze.
Poseidon at play.

Late Summer

The sun sets early
Yet still muggy air prevails
No breezes stir it.

A hawk's eyes and wings
Circle, alertly patrol,
Survey wilted grass.

Dried seed pods have burst
Their contents scattered afield
Empty shells remain.

Insects grow louder
Swarms dart about among branches
Birds' songs are not heard.

In sweat–drenched clothing
Thirsty gardeners sit back
Gulp cold, clear water.

August Morning

Summer's heat slackens
The sun drifts south, sets early
No wind stirs still air.

Asphalt retains heat
Parched brown earth soaks in no rain
Creeks dried weeks ago.

Flowers have wilted
Scents and bright colors faded
Their seeds fall to earth.

Autumn

The Equinox Approaches

Goldenrod flowers
With modest colors, serve as
Autumn's harbinger.

Dull yellow blossoms
Their hues brightening under
The sun's direct gaze

Show us summer's end.
Long early morning shadows
Contrast with gold blooms.

A Season Begins

A fresh stinging gust
Heralding the equinox
Strikes us from the west.

Gray clouds venture east
Rain droplets rush down sideways
Chill leaves, heads, grass, earth.

Autumn's Onset

The September sun
Relents, yet still coaxes leaves
To their fulfillment.

Grains and fruits ripen
Chrysanthemum blooms emerge
Promising bounty.

October Dawn

Intense morning light
Streaming in from the southeast
Highlights turning leaves.

The hard maple's hues
Brighten from green to orange
Matching those of flames.

This brilliant fire
Gives the year a final burst,
A defiant sign.

Soon all will turn brown
But now, leaves and blades of grass
Absorb the sun's rays.

Remembering Paul Verlaine

Yellow autumn leaves,
Their color still brightly shown,
Drift across the field,

Driven by the wind,
Wandering forth, aimlessly,
We follow their course.

Green Leaves in November

Branches stretch upward
Into the gray, shrouded sky
Bare, thin, dark, austere.

Yet green leaves persist
Shrubs near the ground still bear them
Vivid, defiant.

November Hunt

The wolves' eyes focus.
Now they prowl the bleak forest
To strike at twilight.

They hide in silence
To track deer in shades of brown:
Earth, grass, leaves and trees.

No color stands out
Then a wolf's teeth strike a deer
And blood stains the ground.

November Images

A few leaves remain
In spite of wind and cold
To cling to branches.

On early evenings
Cloudy skies that hide the sun
Mute once-bold colors.

Brown muddy meadows
Gradually fade from sight
Under thin gray mists.

Late Autumn Warm Spell

Mid-November winds
Push rain and warmth from the south
Then display the sun.

Zephyrs fly about
Soaked leaf carpets slowly dry
Weather vanes must shift.

The gentle sunlight
Offers a glimpse of summer.
Soon the winds will turn.

Autumn's Last Moments

Calm December air
Beneath a dim gray curtain
Lets barren trees rest.

This year's storms ended
Soaked soil still shows green grass
Interspersed with mud.

The north wind pauses
Sunlight drifts further southward
Cold blasts slowly form.

Mermaids

A Mermaid Amuses Herself

He thought he grasped her
Yet soon she swam to the depths
Waves pushed him ashore.

Mermaids Grin

It was quite easy
His thoughts were quickly divined
How he could be lured.

Mermaid Mischief

The yacht seemed secure
Captain and crew were alert
And the sea was calm.

The formal dinner
With its maritime setting
Started pleasingly.

Finely-coiffed ladies
Silk dresses and velvet gloves
Showed off elegance.

Refined gentlemen
Chose truly perfect outfits:
Dry-cleaned tuxedos.

From waiters' white gloves
Well-blended cocktails were served
The band struck up tunes.

In the depths below
Mermaids finalized their plans
As dinner began.

Wartime explosives
Can detonate just enough
When used properly.

A delicate touch
Made the bomb stick to the hull
And then it went off.

It was a small bomb
The yacht rose only a bit
Nobody was hurt.

All seemed in order
No need to stop the party
The fish course arrived.

The captain chatted
Allowed no interruptions
Had more champagne poured.

And yet belowdecks
The crew could not plug the hole
Although ordered to.

A list was noticed
One tilting to the port side
And not the guest list.

The mermaids giggled
They had found the yacht's weak spot
Now the coup de grace.

In Orca fashion
They assembled to make waves
Fins in unison.

Formed in a long line
In well-synchronized motion
They caused waves to crest.

Pushed by foam masses
And revealing its paint job
The starboard side rose.

Trays and tables tipped
Soon the guests tumbled as well
Food stained formal clothes.

Alert rescuers
Could not bring their boats too close
It was time to jump.

Startled revelers
Applied their swimming lessons
Rings were tossed to them.

None of them were lost
It was a simple soaking
No one missed dinner.

The mermaids swam off
What a charming prank to pull
No one guessed a thing.

Mermaids

Splashing, frolicking
In shallow waters near rocks
Singing playful songs.

A quick plunge downward
With fins swaying back and forth
To explore bright reefs.

Their hands uncover
Prey open oysters, snatch pearls
Treasures in the depths.

Swift, graceful, agile
They find gems, delicacies,
Swim without restraint.

Far from sailors' eyes
They live content, quite heedless
No storms bother them.

Infrequent Meeting

In fading sunlight
He wanders amid eddies
Begins the night's swim.

Though others would drown
He lets the sea push him forth
His heart beats calmly.

On this moonless night
His eyes will perceive nothing
Only trust guides him.

Soon he hears her voice
Reassuring, inviting,
He swims farther still.

Her hands touch his feet
She places him on her back.
Carries him onward.

He holds her gently
She would never cast him off
He understands her.

She knows his story:
Disowned by his family
Dishonored, punished,

Confused, abandoned,
Ever the forlorn beggar
He ekes out a life.

For a few minutes
He knows he will find solace
In this mermaid's arms.

She loves this outcast
Only sees him in secret
Here, far out to sea.

She asks to kiss him
Promises to protect him
Love him faithfully.

Ars Poetica

The Muse

The Muse Needs Not Weep

"My poets must weep
Wander aimlessly in tears
Sigh in deep sorrow.

Those sensitive boys
Very prone to deep despair
Let their wounds spout blood.

They must blame themselves
Give free rein to their remorse
Express their minds' grief.

When their wits return
Happiness will elude them
Gloom will keep its hold.

Their words I will blend
In the midst of their regret
Sweet music will sound."

Music at Midnight

A weary poet
Hears soft, calm, soothing music
A soprano voice.

The Muse has returned
To sing quiet melodies
Awaken his heart.

The poet sits up
She enchants him yet again
His eyes open wide.

The Muse Takes My Hand

The Muse takes my hand
Stares laughingly in my eyes
Refuses to speak.

Her eyes turn away
A nightingale enchants her
His songs make her weep.

From the bird's calm heart
His song's notes echo gently
Coax me to silence.

She views me again
Hears only the nightingale
Begs me to listen.

Inadvertently Divulged

Her eyes seem to drift
Focus on a distant dream
As she slowly speaks:

"The best ones are boys,
Agèd boys, perhaps, but boys,
Boys I coax to dream.

With grace, songs, dances,
I easily dazzle them
My caprice guides them.

I make no demands
Flatter, entice, inveigle
Grin, laugh, soothe, beguile.

Simple instructions
Disciplined works then follow
They wish to please me

I unleash their minds
Joyful ecstasy bursts forth
Colorful, boundless.

Exuberance fades
Sadness brings out mournful tears
And joy does return.

Forward I lead them
Sharpen their wits and senses
Have you not noticed?"

The Muse stops speaking
Does not see anyone else
A boy approaches.

The Insight She Offers

"I judge as I please
Maintain no rules, no program,
Offer random clues.

I seek wanderers
Draw them into my circle
Let their minds spout dreams.

Those delightful boys
Beautiful, charming, witty,
How they obey me.

Very few please me
Though they enjoy my favor
I will discard them."

Frolicking Spirit

The Muse is alone
No one to hear her singing
Nor see her dancing

She never tires
Boundless, endless energy
Restless, capricious

Graceful, untamed steps
Songs of deep sorrow, then joy
Laughter, profuse tears

Frenetic whirlwind
Speeds on new paths she chooses
Far from human eyes.

The Muse Must Frolic

The Muse must frolic
Raise her voice in pleasing songs
Dance and leap about.

She laughs at poets
Her poor, dull-witted suitors
Yet begs them to write.

She ignores their pain
Truly wants to delight them
Coax, lure, cajole, prod.

Their minds race forward
Upward to summits, then descend
Amid dark ravines.

Yes, poets stumble
Melancholy strikes some down
They yield to despair.

It sometimes happens
A poet cannot go on
He takes his own life.

Still, the Muse dances
She sheds tears, tears of sorrow
Tinged with tenderness.

Her songs never stop
A brief moment of mourning
The tempo picks up.

No, she is not cruel
Nothing weighs down this spirit
Her feet leave no prints.

Flesh and blood weaken
Worn out by her frantic steps
Their words, though, live on.

Vital Lesson

The Muse instructs me
Tells me to forget myself
Leads me to the sea.

Above jagged rocks
Foam-tipped waves lunge to the shore
She tells me to stare.

Harsh winds sting my face
Salt spray shoots up to strike me
Waves topple sailboats.

"Feel the earth pulsate
Untamed, violent, fertile
Its elements clash.

Your breath, your heartbeat
Have those same fierce elements
Strong yet erratic.

As waves can crush ships
So can you be quickly killed
Death must claim all life."

We sit in silence
Currents carry to the land
Scattered life jackets.

Days of Silence

No poems today?
The Muse prefers not to speak.
Respect her silence.

Take time to ponder
As she calmly meditates
Prepare to listen.

Your calm, relaxed heart
Freed of the world's distractions
Can welcome her words.

Encounter

The Muse visits me
This cool September morning
Twilight yields to day.

Sunbeams reach the ground
Reveal thin, gray shrouds of mist
Above dew-soaked grass.

She calmly sits down
Beckons me to rest my mind
Let my eyes observe.

Light and shadows play
Colors, green, yellow, black, brown,
Contrast bright and dark.

She remains silent
Gives no sign of what she thinks
We scan the landscape.

An Astounding Situation

The Muse fell silent?
She loves attentive poets
Eager to hear her.

She flirts with poets
Drawing forth their gentle sighs
And rhythmic verses.

Now she remains mute
She even begins to sulk
Quiet and alone.

Poetastery

Another Debacle

Lurking in dark bogs
Your poetic nemesis
Concocts fiendish plots.

Rich glittering bait
Lures you away from firm earth
Your toes squish smooth mud.

Bright lights burn brighter
Bedazzle your vacant eyes
Ah, they enchant you.

How you must advance
What superb beings await
See, they beckon you.

Musicians, maidens,
A dancing colorful host
Revelers, jesters.

As at ancient feasts
Bacchanalian delights
Lead you to pleasure.

You strain eagerly
If only you could join them
You would capture bliss.

Hear their joyful song
You have success at hand then
Fall face-first in mud.

Though you thrash about
The bog keeps you in its grip
You lie on your back.

Reclining in mud
You find your place for the night
The full moon rises.

With dawn's arrival
I see you barely moving
Let me pull you out.

The Poetry Scene at Times

The Muse pulls a prank
Beckons complacent poets
Gives out words of praise.

With a demon's wit
She offers rewards to them
Promises glory.

She shows them a world
Glittering with vast treasures
Bids them to race hence.

Into a morass
Befuddled poets lunge fast
Slow to a wallow.

Sturdy illusions
Convince them of eloquence
Fill their minds with hope.

The Muse sings loud songs
Goads the poets to press on
Slither if need be.

Three paces onward
Heedless of muck that covers
Efforts still persist.

The Muse stops singing
This gag is simply too much!
What poems emerge!

Belabored nonsense
Uplifted buffoonery
Drawn from a deep pit.

The Muse loves to laugh
How easily she tricks us
Lures us yet again.

Culinary

Breakfast

Scorched in a hot pan
Runny eggs become solid
But drip with butter.

Bacon fat softens
White color gives way to gray
The rest is charred red.

Crispy, toasted bread
Is smeared with butter and jam
Turns brown, yellow, red.

Soft, darkened home fries
Neatly sliced potato cubes
Give peppered flavor.

Flowing through the grounds
Black coffee, thick and heavy,
Slowly fills the pot.

Plump, pressed oranges
Yield sweet undiluted juice
With small bits of pulp.

Look out the window
At the wind-driven drizzle
Work will soon begin.

Starbucks

Paris it is not.
No ornate surroundings
No well-dressed waiters.

Wait your turn in line
No leisurely service here
Maybe you can sit.

No cups or saucers
Sip from paper or plastic
Do find the trash can.

As for the coffee?
True, true, they know how to brew,
The machines work well.

All throughout the land
Each place looks like the others
Standards are upheld.

Yes, they sell good stuff,
I do like stopping in, but,
Paris it is not.

Give Me Some Heavy Food

Cholesterol please,
Scrambled eggs, bacon, sausage
Butter-covered toast.

Later in the day
T-Bone steak with the fat on
With hollandaise sauce.

Don't forget dessert
Tiramisu with sugar
And some heavy cream.

Some "unhealthy" meals
May clog our arteries
But let's take a chance.

Dinner

Close the heavy door
Let cold winds lash against it
Take off your soaked coat.

The table is set
Plate and silverware in place
Cocktails are ready.

Tonight a sidecar
Brandy and Cointreau mingle
Sweet smooth subtle strong.

No salad for you
Look at what we let simmer
Then deftly covered.

Steaming onion soup
Topped by a thick cheese layer
Slowly pierce and savor.

Wait a moment please,
The main course is not ready
Cooking duck does take time.

Although hot inside
The tender meat remains red
And we trimmed no fat.

A sugary sauce
Dripped here and there on the plate
Hints of spring berries.

Modest garnishings
Carrots, potato bits, peas,
Sprinkled with pepper.

A simple dessert
A bit of chocolate mousse
Heaped by the spoonful.

As dinner winds down
Enjoy a sip of cognac
Your warm bed awaits.

Salmon on the Grill

A soaked cedar plank
Beneath a slab of salmon
Slowly absorbs heat.

Charcoal glows orange
Black lumps are consumed in flames
Make smoke, steam mingle.

Spices melt, then spread
As salmon's color lightens
Fat drops ooze downward.

Fifteen minutes pass.
Taste soft, moist, sweetened morsels
That blend flame, wood, steam.

Lobster for Dinner

Take out your hammer
Crack the heavy armor plate
Open your lobster,

Tough yet delicate
Slightly sweet, barely seasoned
A hint of butter.

Rip open the claws
Eat the lobster's softest flesh:
The red-speckled hands.

After you finish
Armor pieces fill your plate
Remains of dinner.

Lenten Observance

Lent has come again,
We all binged, we all gained weight
Now we must abstain.

No more heavy food
Leave out cream, butter, grease, eggs
Enjoy something else.

Come to the table.
After the salad, we serve
Lightly grilled scallops.

Some olive oil
Blends with vinegar, softens
Its partner's harshness.

Fresh, green, crisp, drenched leaves
Spiced with sweet onions, carrots
Give subtle flavor.

A hot metal grill
Quickly sears plump sea scallops:
The main course tonight.

Brown rice, peas, sea salt
Offer simple harmony
To firm, smooth scallops.

Blood orange dessert
Then you can sit back, content,
Ponder God's wisdom.

No Booze

A toast to binging
With excessive Haiku verse
No booze, just poems.

No wine for me now
Not that I don't like it, but
No beer or spirits.

I think I'll sample
Something else, that refreshes,
Maybe some fruit juice

Orange or grapefruit
Or some kind of berry juice
With lemon slices

Then perhaps some tea
Matcha brewed to a deep green
Color of pea soup

Later in the day
Clear, chilled mineral water
Sparkling in the glass.

As I take a sip,
I already think about
Tomorrow's coffee.

Wine in the future?
Of course, I will take a glass
Well, maybe next week.

Bacchus

Offering your wine
Sparkling, red, rosé, or white
Since antiquity

Chubby god of wine
A mischievous connoisseur
Tapping old barrels

Your world have may passed
Your spirit, though, lives on
Here in Avignon.

You always remain
Gourmet, gourmand, reveler,
Yet a taskmaster.

You demand hard work
Before allowing a feast,
And we need some luck.

First comes spring pruning
Removing the weaker wood
Then training the vines.

Watching the leaves grow
The sun then ripens the grapes
Expectations rise.

Hazards always lurk
Damp weather, mildew, aphids,
Then a lost harvest.

After the summer heat
Comes the time to pluck ripe grapes.
This year has been good.

Tradition explains
Vintners learn anew each year
To blend, let ferment.

When the cork pops out
And the glass fills up with wine
We respect your art.

Generous Bacchus
Our honored guest, faithful friend
Welcome to dinner.

We pour in your glass
Smooth, dry Châteauneuf-du-Pape
With a light bouquet.

Your sensitive nose
Recognizes this vintage
A votre santé!

Suspense

Night in the Suburbs

The sun slowly sets
Then tranquilly the night falls
On our relaxed town.

Locked doors, locked windows
Keep the outside world at bay
At least we think so.

What happens at home?
The houses look peaceful, calm,
No hint of discord.

Behind all the walls
Trouble is always stirring
We keep it hidden.

On your nighttime walks
You will have no inkling
Of what goes on here.

Alfred Hitchcock Advertises

We keep the murders
Solely in the family
In this suspense film.

You will feel a fright
When the memories return
Many weeks from now

Realizing how
Vulnerable you can be
When you least expect.

No, you are not safe.
The villain will soon find you
At some unknown time.

Oh, it's just a film
An imaginary tale
But, please, lock the doors.

Alfred Hitchcock Closes the Shades

Peer out your window
See all the activity
Neighbors work and play.

Things sometimes seem strange.
What is that man carrying?
Where has his wife gone?

You keep peeking in.
You might see something, you know,
Something quite dreadful.

Careful how you watch.
When you feel safe in your room,
Someone might look back.

A Fortune Quickly Earned

Cute, witty, well-dressed
She seized the divorced man's heart
Lured him to her place.

With help from YouTube
She made their love story known
The world was impressed.

Days spent setting up
Followed by passionate nights
Led to a wedding.

Ever the good sport
He did not mind the scandal
Love has its rewards.

People were happy
All celebrated, except,
His gray-haired daughters.

A Fortune Quickly Lost

A wealthy heiress
Privileged, relaxed, at ease
Leads an ordered life.

Servants come promptly
All meals at regular times
Garments cleaned and pressed.

Well-kept bank accounts
Contain long lists of figures
All pennies counted.

Content with her lot
She asks little of others
At least, not too much.

One late afternoon
She lifts her porcelain cup
Sips tea with sugar.

Her eyes go bleary
Breathing becomes arduous
Her head tilts downward.

Startled servants stare
Yet no white gloves will touch her
No request comes forth.

Anxious moments pass.
Someone panics, looks about,
Sees a telephone.

Emergency please
The heiress has fallen pale
We cannot explain.

Inquiries will show
Well, hopefully, what happened
Is someone to blame?

The covered heiress
Is taken out, silently,
Doctors write reports.

It soon becomes clear:
Her banker forged her will, and,
Understood strychnine.

A Man of Confidence

Such a smooth talker
Yes, Bernie could close the deal
Profits guaranteed.

His wealthy clients
Eagerly planned their futures
They placed trust in him.

Their friends approached him
They too, wanted to invest
Invest with Madoff.

All was going well
The balance sheets all looked good
Then the crisis hit.

Sorry about that
No even breaks for suckers
Your money is gone.

Caught Unaware

On a sunlit beach
She chills out, luxuriates
A cocktail arrives.

Fluffy clouds pass by
On the rich azure canvas
Seagulls slowly glide.

Small waves push surfers
Who sway along the currents
Drift onto the sand.

An angler's work ends
He has pulled out a prize fish
A fine new conquest.

Swimmers splash around
White foam masses caress them
Swirl in the shallows.

The sun moves westward
Slowly the sky will turn red
She feels most content.

A young man hurries
He must bring her a message
The front desk insists.

The note on the tray
Tells her how she must check out
Her rich lover left.

Do Watch Out

Such a careful plot
Eliminates evidence
The crime should succeed.

Velvet gloves, dark clothes
Worn, non-streaking tennis shoes
Sharp weapon concealed.

Alarm disabled
Money, jewels, credit cards
Victims unaware.

Later, a quick sale
This loot commands a high price
Some crook will pay it.

Sneak through dark hallways
Nothing left to find back there
See the side exit.

What, the lights come on?
Greetings from the police chief
Someone tipped him off.

Grounds for Gossip

Yes, the old widow,
The one in the big mansion,
She lives quite content.

What was her story?
Does she talk about the past?
She seems so discreet.

Of modest background
She worked unobtrusively
Gained others' favor.

Her boss's poor wife
Suddenly fell deathly ill
She comforted him.

At the funeral,
She shed copious tears
Mourned the departed.

A mournful year passed
She consoled a widower
Spoke of happy times.

The sad man cheered up
He knew he found a new love
And proposed marriage.

She gladly agreed
Soon, her entire life changed:
No longer modest.

A society queen
With entourage close by
She reigned serenely.

Strange, though, how he died
Her robust husband took ill
Yes, she still sheds tears.

Money Circulates

The executive
Delegates all decisions
Orders wheels to turn.

Smooth operations
Epitomize his business
Progress rapidly.

Quarterly profits
Recorded regularly
Prove his acumen.

Along with his work
He pursues refined pleasures
Food, wine, art, ladies.

The Ritz in Paris
Welcomes him and chosen guest
Quite a smart couple.

His gorgeous mistress
Is first somewhat ill at ease
Soon very relaxed.

Before he returns
She asks to stay in Paris
The shops await her.

He resumes his work
Then a small memo arrives:
A bank inquiry.

A flight to Rio,
But first, from all his accounts
A transfer of funds.

Sir, we are sorry
See, here is your signature
She did not forge it?

In her hotel room
She hangs up on his lawyer
Her boyfriend laughs too.

Our Court System

Yes, Dominick Dunne
Knew what people are up to
And get away with.

Murder charges clear-cut
There's plenty of evidence
Why plead innocent?

Our justice system
Gives the wealthy what they seek:
Acquittal for sale.

High priced attorneys
Create a courtroom circus
Toss out evidence.

Busy reporters
Achieve tabloid perfection
Look good on TV.

Befuddled judges
Stare blankly, glassed-eyed, confused,
Cameras show them.

When the verdict comes
The poor DA shakes his head
It happens again.

Those rich defendants
They sure got their money's worth
Verdict: not guilty.

The travesty ends
We have one consolation:
The gossip goes on.

Sunset Years

The widow's accounts
Checking, savings, investments
Took care of her needs.

Her deceased husband
Gave her the house, car, servants
Plus medical care.

With weekly payments
Approved by her signature
She gave salaries.

Her ample fortune
With more than sufficient funds
Freed all from worry.

A daily routine
Made all the staff feel secure
She enjoyed each day.

Her thoughtful old nurse
Had studied all her habits
Knew which pills to give.

Two pills to relax
The old widow fell asleep
Slept longer each night.

She slowly weakened
But still thanked her busy nurse
Since she felt no pain.

When her time ran out
The staff could read with pleasure
Her generous will.

Dona Nobis Pacem

War Afflicts our World

War afflicts our world
Random murder and bloodshed
The scourge of our time

No armies in ranks
Just sporadic explosions
Maiming and killing

Serving no purpose
Ending lives before their time.
When will peace arrive?

More Reports of War

More reports of war
Civilians killed and wounded
Car bombs in markets

Fearful people flee
Refugees remain in camps
Hoping to survive

The appeals for peace
Will fall on deaf ears today
As bombs detonate

Doctors rush to help
To save the mass of wounded
In smoke-stained ruins

While a martyr waits
Sees the ambulance and crew
Then a bomb goes off.

A Feckless Demonstration

Combative Ares
Views the protesters with scorn
Cannot respect them.

Their weary slogans
Pompous bleating for world peace
Repeat and repeat.

Indulged citizens
Will never withstand combat
Fear no enemies.

No squalor, no pain
No discomfort, all needs met
Meals at proper times,

Their convenient lives
Allow them to leave their homes
March, tweet, return home.

Ares, disgusted,
Will not suffer such dullards
Unknown to battle.

Cruel, eager Ares
Knows who are taking up arms
He will not wait long.

Combat via Satellite

More war on TV
We find it clean, sanitized
Just more news reports

Like watching movies
We sit in our comfy homes
Nothing bothers us

No stench of corpses
No wounded screaming for help
Only news broadcasts

We soon tire of it
Something else must be on now
Let's change the channel.

An Appeal for Peace

An appeal for peace
Comes from members of clergy
Of different faiths

Yet the bombs explode
The bullets fly into crowds
The body count grows.

We hear of the need
For peace in our bloodied world
But war continues.

Weeping and mourning
Are the order of the day
Just like yesterday.

News We Do Not Understand

Where is Samara?
Somewhere in southern Iraq,
A shrine once stood there.

Newscasts give reports
Some Sunnis, fighting Shiites,
Blew the thing sky-high.

The experts argue
About al-Qaida, the war,
And what it all means.

A beautiful shrine
This noteworthy masterpiece
Reduced to rubble.

More TV debates
With no one understanding
What to make of it.

The loss of artwork
Of such great architecture
Makes experts babble.

How can we remain
So blasé and ignorant
Of this suffering?

Do we not notice
The great loss to all of us
Of life and beauty?

Then other newscasts
Relate some story elsewhere.
We change the channel.

Another Marketplace Bombing in Baghdad

Down's Syndrome children
Loving, trusting and docile,
With no evil thoughts

Told to carry bombs
Sent out into the large crowd
Just doing as told.

From a safe distance
Mass murder is committed
By remote control.

Simply flick the switch.
The bombs go off, people die.
A gruesome plan worked.

Down's Syndrome children
Those children, now made martyrs
Did not guess a thing.

Scarcely a protest,
Leaders simply deem this act
Only more killing.

Yes, Each Day Is a Poem

You are right, Jeffers,
In how you described a day:
Painful to excess.

Yours words resonate
The blood, the omens, the wars,
Earthquake and red moon.

Tyrants will still wail
In wrath and dog wrath, genius
Cored on sick child souls.

We see their faces
Glaring, furious, vengeful,
Cynical, spiteful.

The news program ends.
In fading daylight I see
Hawks amid red clouds.

Remembrance

Each Eleventh of November

Many years have passed
The last veterans have died
Yet we remember.

Photographs and films
Show generals and marshals
The High Command's staff.

Common soldiers' words
Try to relate the events
Offer us a glimpse.

Battlefield markers
Starting points for offensives
Recall H-Hours.

Some postwar pictures
Of scarred, crippled, dazed people
Jar our memories.

Much has been rebuilt
Our world's progress continues
Yet we remember.

Commémoration

A simple poilu
Filthy, profane, violent
The war's real hero,

Not Joffre, not Foch,
Not Mangin, not Clemenceau,
Not the officers.

Respect the poilu.
Ready to fight or rebel
He saved his country.

Visit battlefields
Verdun or Chemin des Dames
Remember this man.

Think back to that time
Your mind can hear sounds of a
Dying man wailing.

To Helmut Johannes von Moltke

It seemed so urgent
You felt the need to strike fast
While you could still win.

Early September
You hoped to enter Paris
It was not to be.

Hentsch gave you reports
Kluck and Bülow must retreat
Defeat on the Marne.

Relieved of command,
You returned home a failure
Dead soon afterwards.

Today we think back
It looks quaint, all those men in
Their Pickelhauben.

On the battlefields
Tourists read guidebooks, matching
Map signs to landmarks.

Tranquil country fields
Only traces remain of
The war to end wars.

Yet we remember
All: Feldgrau, Tommy, Poilu
Worthy of respect.

At length we reflect
These days we hear reports of
Those who rush to war.

HMS Prince of Wales

A white ensign waves
Lowered onto the gravesite:
Twisted steel, blood, tears.

Each Sixth of June

Calm Norman morning,
Tourists view the landing site,
Trace the battles' course,

Slowly they advance,
View obstacles, cliffs, bunkers,
Then, names of the dead.

Papers

The second plane hit
A fireball, smoke, panic
Then, all the papers,

Fluttering downward
Policies, memos, reports,
Agendas, archives,

Drifting east and north
Reviewed, dated, approved, signed,
Put into effect.

Now, out of our reach
Transactions, accomplishments,
No records remain.

Lower Manhattan, Autumn 2001

Although weeks have passed
Smoke keeps billowing upward
Gray, acrid, toxic,

Drifting with the winds
Ash and particles scatter
Fall on earth and sea.

Beneath jagged steel
Compounds seep, blend, and ignite
More smoke clouds will rise.

Slowly, bit by bit,
Fragments are taken away
The cleanup begins.

The city's heart beats
Fights back, persists and pulsates,
Yet scars will remain.

My Next Pilgrimage

Near the finished towers
Manhattan's tallest, toughest
Great accomplishments.

You will see me there
A tourist among tourists
Checking out the sites.

Soon, though, I will stop
Completely ignore the crowds
See the monuments.

You can stare at me
Simply do not speak to me
Do not speak at all.

I will read the names
Name after name after name
You must hear them all.

As my voice weakens
My eyes will not stop weeping.
Yet still I must speak.

Listen to each name
Remember with me that day
I see you weeping.

Our tears do not stop
Take my hand, guide me homeward
When I have finished.

Mark Schardine is a New Jersey resident with a
lifelong love of poetry. In 2015, he published a French
language book of his poems, entitled *Au bord des rêves*,
and in 2019, it was followed by *Vers des horizons
lointains*, and his first English language book *Charm,
Elegance, and Intrigue*.

Previous Publications:

Au bord des rêves, Editions Mélibée, 2015

Vers des horizons lointains, Editions Baudelaire, 2019

Charm, Elegance, and Intrigue, Red Dashboard LLC, 2019

www.ingramcontent.com/pod-product-compliance
Lightning Source LLC
Chambersburg PA
CBHW062059270326
41931CB00013B/3146